"What Do They Mean When They Say…?"

Decoding Performance Evaluation Speak

Deborah Gray-Young

Copyright © 2018 Deborah Gray-Young

All rights reserved.

ISBN:13:978-0692963029
ISBN-10:0692963022

DEDICATION

To working women everywhere, but especially to our Hidden Figures© - Black women who often endure glass ceilings, brick walls and insults beyond reason and comprehension.

"When they go low, we go high!"
Michelle Obama

"And Still I Rise!"
Maya Angelou

"What Do They Mean When They Say...?"

TABLE OF CONTENTS

	Acknowledgments	vii
Chapter	Introduction	9
1	You're Not Politically Savvy	11
2	You're Not A Team Player	15
3	You're Not A Good Fit	19
4	We'll Pay You, But Won't Promote You	23
5	Some People Are Intimidated by You	29
6	Your Brand is Getting Too Big	33
	Part 2	37
7	How Do Others View You, Really?	39
8	What's Your RQ?	43
9	Developing A Stakeholder Map	45
10	Always Be A Student of Your Craft	47

TABLE OF CONTENTS,

11	Want To Be Taken Seriously?	51
12	Who's Holding Your Ladder?	55
13	About That LinkedIn Profile	61
14	A Final Word	65
	About the Author	67
	Books by D. Gray-Young	69
	D. Gray-Young Webinars and Workshops	71
	What People Say About Deborah	73

"What Do They Mean When They Say…?"

ACKNOWLEDGMENTS

Thank you to my two super fans, sounding boards, and sanity anchors:

My husband Gerald Young who always gives excellent feedback and suggestions and has patience Job would envy.

Betty Clayton, former boss and friend of over 30 years. Betty is my truth teller and believes in my talent and capability, especially on those days when I do not.

♥

INTRODUCTION

In my work as an executive coach with professional women of color, the question I am asked most is "what do they mean when they say..? It is almost always about their performance evaluation or goal setting discussion.

Just what do they mean when they say, "your work is excellent, but...

- You're not politically savvy
- You're not a team player
- You're not a good fit
- We'll pay you, but will not promote you
- Some People find you intimidating
- Your brand is becoming too big

There are dozens more, I'm sure. In this book, we will explore and discuss the most common of them and provide tips on how to manage the comments and perceptions that accompany each.

Once you have some understanding of what was said, what was meant, what do you do? How do you address it?

Included here are a few chapters from my previous book that you may find helpful as you continue to navigate your corporate experience. Every chapter includes self-coaching questions designed to assist you with thinking through your particular situation and developing strategies to strengthen relationships as well as your personal and professional brand.

Life is fraught with obstacles and seeming roadblocks. I believe in removing all of the barriers that are in our power to do so. That's the purpose of this book; to help you identify, understand and deal with obstacles that are within your power to address. Ultimately, we all want to know that we did all we could; that we did our best. That is the purpose of this book.

I hope you find this book helpful. I would love it if you would share with me know how you use it for your particular situation. Drop me a note. My contact information is on page 71.

Wishing you continued success,

Deborah

Deborah Gray-Young

1 What Do They Mean When They Say "You're Not Politically Savvy"?

This is one of the most common comments professional women of color get on their performance evaluations: "Your work is excellent, but you're not politically savvy."

What do they mean when they say you're not politically savvy? Well, it could mean a number of things, but almost every time I heard this from a client, she was someone who worked very hard and had developed good technical skills.

However, she had a low threshold for office politics and little regard for the titles and roles of management, executive leadership, and other key stakeholders.

These women were focused solely on the work and meeting deadlines, not on forging relationships or paying attention to their image or how they were perceived within the organization.

Now, to a person, every one of the women I heard this from said, "I don't have time for politics."

Here's where you should make the distinction between politics and foolishness. There is a difference. Political savvy is being aware of the people and the dynamics that can and will impact your career and success trajectory.

Foolishness is non-productive activity engaged in by people with not enough to do (or they are not focused on what they are supposed to be doing). Yes, sometimes it is a fine line, but that's why you are ordained with the power of discernment.

So, what does it mean to be politically savvy and how do you acquire it?

For starters, being politically savvy entails, you understanding who all of the people and positions are that impact your experience and trajectory within your organization.

Knowing who the people are is important because understanding personalities, as well as management and leadership styles, are essential. Also, it would help if you understood the function of the positions within the organization that can influence your career path; people rotate in out of positions all of the time, but the function most likely remains on the org chart.

Here are some questions for you to consider:

1. What is the mission or primary objective of the organization and how does what you do help to fulfill that? Another way to ask this is, what value do you contribute to the organization?

2. How are you perceived within your organization? Your image is more than how you look.

3. Where are you positioned in the current organizational structure?

"What Do They Mean When They Say…?"

4. Where do you aspire to move?

5. How have you developed relationships with key stakeholders beyond your immediate level of management?

On the next page is a copy of the Six Steps to Becoming Politically Savvy*, also available on my website as a free download. Visit http://www.coachdgrayyoung.com/free-e-book-download/

Six Steps to Becoming Politically Savvy

1. Get clear about what you want to achieve within the organization. Don't sit around hoping that a promotion or stretch assignment will just happen. Hope ain't a strategy.

2. Develop mini dossiers. Identify the people within your organization that you should know. Who are they and what are their interests? You are looking for common ground to start a conversation and gradually begin to build a professional relationship. LinkedIn is the best place to start. There's also the subtle but powerful tactic of strategic sharing.

3. Check your communication style. What is your dominant communication style and what are the styles of the people you work with most often?

4. What is your work or management style? Do you work in a silo? Don't share information or effectively delegate assignments? People who work in silos flunk political savvy every time.

5. For what are you the go-to person? Another way to put this is, what are you known for within your organization? If it's shoes or what are the best restaurants, you have some work to do.

6. Develop a keen understanding of the mission, business situation, and objectives of the organization. How does your role contribute to the organization's ability to deliver on those three pillars?

2 WHAT DO THEY MEAN WHEN THEY SAY "YOU'RE NOT A TEAM PLAYER"?

When someone is told they are not being a team player, that can be a stinging criticism. Hopefully, this one is not heard too often. Sometimes being labeled not a team player can be a misperception if the person works in the background or behind the scenes where their contribution to the team is not very visible. Usually, this critique is potentially based on one of four situations:

1. You work in a silo
2. You don't
    a. Cooperate or collaborate well
    b. Delegate effectively
    c. Share information in a timely manner
3. You take credit for team efforts
4. You've been known to throw co-workers under the bus.

Scenarios one, two and three are reversible. Number four, not so much and warrants a whole other discussion that will not be covered here.

How does one reverse the stigma of not being a team player? It will take a little bit of work, but it's doable provided there is no irreversible damage to your reputation.

Let's begin with determining why is it that you are not

considered a team player? Is it based on observation or specific incidents and complaints? The difference is crucial because it will inform the course of action you take to improve your evaluation and the negative perception of you within the organization.

Working in A Silo

There are very few benefits, if any, to working in a silo. My experience has been that when people work in a silo, it suggests one of a number of dynamics, none of which are constructive to a positive career trajectory.

People intentionally work in a silo because:
1. They believe they are the smartest people in the room
2. They are insecure about their knowledge and competency for their position
3. They are an introvert and are more comfortable staying to themselves

If you are the smartest person in the room, then you're probably in the wrong room. You can't learn or be stretched out of your comfort zone. However, rarely are the people who think they are the smartest people in the room, actually the smartest people in the room. If by chance you are, it is an excellent opportunity to lead and share, not gloat and hoard your knowledge and expertise.

If you lack confidence in your ability to perform the responsibilities of your role, become a student of your craft. (Read more about this in chapter 10) Seek out a mentor, or work with an executive coach to help you gain the confidence you need to feel more comfortable with workplace interactions. If you are an introvert, you don't get a free pass here either. As Dan Rockwell, The Leadership Freak notes in his advice for introverts, "Stretch you collaboration muscles."

Lack of Cooperation and Collaboration

When you don't extend yourself to cooperate or collaborate, you deprive yourself of important opportunities to market your thinking and capability internally. You also limit opportunities to learn and establish key relationships with colleagues and stakeholders. Some of you are reluctant to collaborate because of the fear that your ideas will be taken and used without acknowledging your contribution. While that is a legitimate concern, there's very little you can do about someone's lack of integrity. (See my comments on this in the next paragraph) One way to combat this is have more than two people working on the idea and if it is only two people, share the meeting recap notes including ideas presented and expected outcomes to the broader team.

Taking Credit Where Credit Is Not Due

There's not much to say about taking credit for someone else's' ideas and work. It's wrong and speaks volumes about the lack of character and integrity of people who do it. And yet, it happens quite frequently. If the team did the work, give the team the kudos. If a particular team member offered an idea or suggestion that leads to the team's success, then make sure to acknowledge that team member's contribution. The quick-fast shortcut to damaging your reputation is to take credit for ideas or work that are not yours. Also, don't make the mistake of thinking that no one will know the difference. Someone always knows, or a situation will arise that will pierce that veil.

Delegating Effectively

If you lead a team, delegating effectively is a critical component of strong leadership. Delegating assignments effectively means you provide clear direction on what is needed and why the task is important. You also provide all pertinent information available so that the team can proceed efficiently and effectively. There is nothing to be gained by attempting to do everything yourself unless of course, you are a one-person team. Even then, you will need the assistance of someone else to help you successfully fulfill your responsibilities.

Not being a team player is probably not how you want to be branded. It is a dead-end designation that ultimately leads to frustration and not a successful career trajectory. If this is your situation, only you can decide how to move forward.

List three things you can do immediately to begin to reverse the perception that you are not a team player.

1.

2.

3.

3 What Do They Mean When They Say "You're Not A Good Fit"?

Just what does "you're not a good fit" mean?

It could mean a few things and could depend on whether you hear it during the interview process or after you've been hired. In any case, it more than likely relates to any or all of the following, as well as other dynamics:

- Corporate culture
- Management/leadership style
- Perspective

My observation and experience are that this can also be a code that companies hide behind when they do not have the courage to hire someone that is well qualified for a position but is different from their typical profile.

When you are confronted with this statement, you are obligated to yourself to delve deeper and ask questions. Why? Because if for no other reason, you want to know what is at the core of this statement and perception.

You also want the opportunity to discuss it for your own learning. It may be something you can address and adjust. Usually, I advise people that if you hear this in an interview process, be somewhat grateful. There's nothing worse than making a career move and finding out it isn't a fit in any shape, way or form. This usually occurs when the position or the roles and responsibilities have been misrepresented. A colleague experienced this after relocating, no less.

So, what should be your response when you hear "You're not a good fit"? Assuming you are surprised and disagree:

1. Remain calm
2. Put on your "inquiring minds want to know" hat and ask probing open-ended questions. Here are a few to put in your toolkit.

    - I am disappointed to hear that. Can you give me some insight into what specifically doesn't fit?" or
    - All of the conversations I have had seemed to go well and I understood the challenges and expectations. Can you share what is precisely the disconnect?

Asking probing questions does two things:

1. It communicates that you do not agree and
2. You are not going to settle for a vague excuse of not being a fit without the "fit" being qualified

Now, if the person you are speaking with begins to stammer, squirm or breaks into a sweat, you know that it is something they do not want to verbalize that is at the core of this. Make it clear that you are only interested in learning so that you can address and adjust whatever it is, if possible.

Conversely, if you know it's not a good fit, graciously agree and be done with it.

However, if you hear this after you have been hired and/or have worked for the company for a while, there's another set of dynamics that need to be considered and explored. I can't tell you how many times I've heard stories around this.

Women who have risen to VP only to be informed in a performance evaluation that they are not a good fit for the company? Really? Then how did they get that far?

In another scenario, the corporate culture was abusive; the expectation was for people to work 80 hours a week and to do from their sick or dying mother's bed. For the individual that managed their time effectively and fulfilled their assignments on schedule, 80 hours a week did not seem necessary, to say nothing about being unhealthy. The person was informed that they were not a fit; their unwillingness to work 80 hours a week was an indication of their lack of commitment to the company and the client.

In the first case, it was an excuse and perhaps a difference in style. In the second story, it wasn't a fit, and the reason was unreasonable also.

In both cases, at least from where I sit, HR was ineffective in helping these women manage the situations they were facing. Both women ended up leaving their respective positions.

So, when you are told "you're not a good fit," don't be so quick to give in or give up. Press for answers and clarity around what specifically does not fit. You deserve to know.

Here are some tips for being pro-active and managing situations that potentially result in you being told you're not a good fit:

- Don't ignore those intuitive inklings that something isn't right
- Conduct periodic check-ins between performance evaluations to ensure you are tracking toward set goals and expectations
- Ask probing open-ended questions to get to the core issue
- Become an effective team player
- Become politically savvy

4 What Do They Mean When They Say "We Will Pay You But Won't Promote You"?

When the company is willing to pay you, but not promote you, consider it a form of handwriting on the wall. There was a time a decade, or so ago this phrase would have been uttered to keep you out of the "old boys club."

A longtime colleague, years ago, found herself training men as they came into the media department of an advertising agency. After a period of time, the men would get promoted. Finally, my colleague went to the head of the department and pointed out their pattern and said to them, "If you're not going to promote me to VP even though I've trained all of the VPs here, then at least pay me like one." Not wanting to belabor the point, they did just that. Eventually, she did leave and started another successful career.

Today, there is a very high risk of a company being sued if that is the intent and it can be proven. When someone is told "we will pay you, but not promote you, it is usually a sign that there are other issues, perhaps just not with the work.

This scenario can present itself when the feathers of a key stakeholder have been ruffled, or, someone in leadership does not like your style or attitude. There may not be grounds to fire you, but certainly moving up within the organization can be hindered. It also suggests your reputation might be severely damaged.

The issues leading to this scenario most commonly fall in the categories of leadership skills, management style, and interaction with leadership, peers and colleagues.

Unless there is a change in leadership and/or you implement an aggressive strategy to improve your image, this is a situation that is difficult to reverse. Your image is more than how you look.

You probably recognize these as aspects of not being politically savvy, not being a team player, and definitely not being a good fit.

Although this was never my personal experience, I have observed these scenarios two or three times over the course of my career. It was never pretty. What's worse is that everyone else can usually see this scenario unfolding. This is how it usually shows up:

You are good at what you do and have the track record to prove it, but,

- Was it you or you and your team that accomplished the goal?
- Is it you or the team that the client thinks highly of?
- If you manage a team, do the people on the team work for you or with you?
- Do you talk down to direct reports are not important?
- Do you give orders or make requests?

"What Do They Mean When They Say...?"

- Do you dictate what is to be done, or provide instruction and direction for tasks?
- Do things have to be done exactly your way, or do you leave room for people to apply their style and perspective?
- What is the tonality of your internal communication, especially e-mail?
- What is the tenor of your relationships with executive leadership?
- How do people view you, really?

I could go on, but hopefully, you get the point. If you've been told the copany will pay you but will not promote you, there are some things you need to weigh. If any of the above points reflect your situation, then there are changes you should consider making, beginning with defining your leadership skills and style.

While leaving might be inevitable, the truth is, you will take you and your behavior and habits wherever you go, including into your own business. And, you will find yourself repeating this experience yet again.

Have a 360° or EQ (Emotional Intelligence) assessment done and use it as the foundation for personal growth and development strategies.

Flat Organizations.

However, getting paid but not getting promoted does not always signal "handwriting on the wall." There are organizations that are structured to limit the advancement of all but a few. The structure of these organizations would be defined as "flat" and are set up that way to ostensible prevent the company from being top-heavy. "Flat" organizations represent multiple levels of frustration to professionals and their goals for achievement.

The experiences of professionals caught in the "flat" organization web span a range of scenarios:

A manager with 20+ years tenure with responsibility for managing hundreds of millions of dollars and driving strategic direction for a major manufacturer being stymied.

For another colleague, a manager in healthcare delivery, was advised that specific types of responsibilities were required as part of the job description for the next position. Subsequently, additional duties were continuously added, and although fulfilled above expectations, the promotion was never awarded.

In another case, a multiple award-winning managing director struggled to climb to VP while others were hand-picked.

When faced with the dynamics of a "flat organization," there may come a time when you will have to decide whether the title and role is more important than the salary, or the salary more important than the position and title. So much of it will depend on the industry you are in and how far along in your career path you are.

If you have invested a considerable amount of time in the company, you will have to weigh whether leaving to get a role and title more in keeping with your goals offset benefits you might be vested in such as stock options.

"What Do They Mean When They Say...?"

Need-less-to-say, it is critical to understand the organizational structure and the track record for upward mobility on the front-end. A company's veracity as it relates to diversity and career advancement is reflected in their numbers if the company is publicly held. Read the reports. Study the data. Analyze the trends the data indicates. Then proceed with your eyes wide open.

5 What Do They Mean When They Say "Some People Are Intimidated By You"?

I had the privilege of joining a group of dynamic young professional women for breakfast. The program featured an up and coming marketing rock star who was giving the intimate gathering an overview of her road to success.. One of the young women asked the speaker, "How do you handle a situation when someone pulls you to the side and tells you that some of your co-workers feel intimidated by you?"

The speaker gave a great answer, having experienced this herself. I dare say, a lot of professional women of color who are smart, good at what they do and are confident, have heard this in some form or another.

Essentially what the speaker said amounted to not apologizing for being smart and confident which shows up as "Black Girl Swag," she said.

Love it. It so reminded me of the criticism President Obama used to get for being cool. Also, the fact that the First Lady was a Harvard trained lawyer was conveniently ignored in favor of her fashion sensibility. But I digress…

Here's what they really mean when they say some people feel intimidated by you:

They are likely uncomfortable with your confidence and most of all your competence. (Let's be clear. People who are not competent, don't intimidate anybody.)

As women of color, our entrance into a company or organization is not usually because someone made a phone call and got us in. For the most part, it doesn't happen like that for us. Which means, if you are there, you were smart enough and talented enough to at least get in the door. (Surviving is a whole other story, which is why I do the work that I do.)

Towards the end of the breakfast, I asked the young woman who made the complaint. "I don't know," she said. "They wouldn't tell me."

Okay, I thought. "First clue." Then I offered an addendum to the speaker's comments.

When someone says to you that some people feel intimidated by you, it's a code of sorts. You are probably out of context, meaning you are not behaving or performing based on their preconceived idea and expectations of you. The stereotypes ever-present in the media may be the only exposure they have ever had to Black women.

Now, this doesn't let you off the hook entirely. Remember, we want to eliminate or minimize self-imposed obstacles.

Check your communication style. Make sure your tone and attitude towards colleagues and co-workers are not condescending or caustic. This includes written communication. On occasion, I have had the opportunity to review clients' email communication for tone, and sometimes it would make me cringe.

It also goes without saying that you have to be the best at what you do. Always be a student of your craft. Always conduct yourself with dignity and operate with integrity.

"What Do They Mean When They Say...?"

There will always be detractors. Make sure you are not providing them with ammunition.

For the record, Dictionary.com cites intimidation as "to overawe or cow, as through the force of personality or by superior display of wealth, talent, etc."

Restating some points from previous chapters that are applicable here as well, here are some things to consider:

- If you lead a team, how do you feel about the members of the team?

- Do you give orders or make requests?

- Who or what is your leadership style modeled after?

- Do you provide answers and solutions to every situation, or do you allow others to think through ideas to reach a viable result?

In part 2 of this book, Chapter 7, "How Do Others View You, Really?" will provide more insight and additional questions for you to consider.

6 What Do They Mean When They Say "Your Brand is Getting Too Big"?

Your brand is getting too big can be viewed one of two ways:

1. You are becoming well known in your field as an expert and consistently called on to speak at industry events or quoted in industry and business media.

2. You are a well-known corporate figure, and your personal story is compelling and making headlines on its own.

When your story makes you a celebrity, it requires a balancing act.

If you are employed, remember that you represent the company you work for even on your own time. Check your employee manual under the moral clause or code of conduct. The personal and corporate balancing act is especially true if you are a vice president or higher. As a vice president, you are an officer of the company which may afford you some privileges, but may also curtail what you can do on your own time. Be clear about the policies and guidelines that pertain to personal public appearances.

Both types of situations require careful balancing and managing.

Each of us has a story about how we landed where we are in life and our careers. Some of our stories are compelling. They are stories of defied odds, unexpected innovation, well-defined intentions manifesting into incredible success. Every now and again, and perhaps more often now due to social media and the proliferation of independent publishing platforms, our stories are making their way to audiences and often creating sizeable followings for individuals.

For others, it might be a project or cause that you have a lot of passion for.

Your personal story or project may be getting too much attention for someone within the company. The question is whether that attention is favorable to the company's reputation or not. That is what they would/should be most worried.

The exposure may also create jealousy among co-workers and colleagues. You may shrug this off and not consider it essential, but remember, your image is more than how you look. How other people view you is crucial. If you are perceived as only interested in the spotlight and not as committed to the team and the mission, these are kernels of resentment that eventually fester into jealousy and discord.

This is problematic whether you are an independent contributor or a team leader. Either way, it makes for a very awkward environment in which to contribute and lead effectively.

If you are representing the company, your detailed personal story is off limits unless you are illustrating how the said company is a champion of people who have had your experience. Otherwise, it is not advisable to mix the two.

For personal appearances as well as blogging and writing articles on personal topics, your bio and introduction

"What Do They Mean When They Say...?"

should not mention the company you work for or your role at the company.

This should be obvious, but, I'll include it here for the record. Personal speaking engagements should not be conducted on company time.

Here are some simple guidelines that can help you balance your corporate responsibilities and your personal public brand. Try always to be mindful of the impact and implications of your actions:

- When it comes to the notoriety and publicity, what are you looking to gain or leverage from the exposure?
- Are you an official spokesperson for the company?
- Are you presenting a company POV or a personal POV on an industry topic?
- If a personal POV, is it in line with the company's mission and objectives?
- How often have you spoken on the same topic in front of the same audience?
- If discussing your personal story in your professional capacity, how does it relate to your current employer?
- Who else in the company might your publicity and exposure impact? A sponsor? A mentor?

PART 2

Now that you have some understanding of what was meant when they said what they said, what can and should you do to address the comments? Often, a minor course correction is all that is needed.

That course correction can take on many forms, including:

- Gaining clarity around your career and life goals
- A better understanding of how others view you
- Consciously managing your communication style and the response to those you interact with most often
- Developing and strengthening relationships with key stakeholders

This next section includes a few chapters from my previous books that will be helpful to you. Self-coaching questions and exercises are also provided.

"What Do They Mean When They Say...?"

7 How Do Others View You, Really?

Is your professional image what it should be or what it needs to be? Another way to ask this is, how do others really view you? Are you being perceived the way you think you are? More importantly, are you being perceived the way you want?

Your image is more than how you look. Your professional image is about your work and management style and your attitude. Your style and attitude are about the energy you display. A significant part of your image is how people (in this case, your peers, colleagues, and executive leadership) view you. How they regard or consider you have to do with the level and quality of energy, you consistently display.

There are mainly four communication styles and depending on the source or assessment tool; they have different labels: Direct, Indirect, Open and Closed.

In an article "Black Women @ Work" in the November 2014 issue of Essence Magazine, writer Tanisha Sykes discusses four basic communication styles - with clever labels - that are present in the workplace: The Isolated Achiever, the Dutiful Conversationalist, the Safe Communicator, and the Expressive Connector.

Not sure what your communication style is? Take a communication style assessment to assist you in figuring it out. Not only is it important to know what your dominant communication style is, but you also need to know and understand the communication style of those you work with most closely, including direct reports, colleagues and executive leadership.

If you are a team leader, supervisor or manager, how do you regard those on your team? Do they work with you or for you? There is a difference, and the truth of your attitude towards the people on your team makes a big difference in how you are perceived.

Every one of these dynamics plays a part in how you are perceived and whether you are taken seriously or not. If you haven't already, get a handle on how others really view you. A 360° assessment provides invaluable feedback for this. If your organization does not provide 360° evaluations, work with an executive coach to coordinate and facilitate one for you. It is well worth the investment.

Also, gain a greater understanding of your communication style and how you are perceived by others. This will enable you have better control of your image and its impact on your career trajectory. My work with clients almost always begins with an assessment of some type; 360°, DISC or Emotional Intelligence. Starting with an assessment helps them see how they are showing up and serves as the foundation for building success strategies. Assessments are invaluable for informing conscious choices about how to respond to the myriad situations one encounters.

In the final analysis, while ultimately you cannot control what others think about you, you can control how you show up. How you show up can significantly influence how you are perceived.

"What Do They Mean When They Say...?"

As the authors of "The Little Black Book of Success" note, "what people perceive is what they usually believe."

Are you conscious of your emotional energy at work, particularly when interacting with others? Why is this important? It is important because people can feel your energy. Your energy precedes you. That pop culture colloquialism "I feel you" is not just a flippant phrase. It's science.

Your energy signature precedes you and shows up in everything you do including how you dress. Your energy level presents itself in your voice, your communication style and your facial expressions and body language.

Your energy is also reflected in your listening skills and how well you listen. Your listening skills demonstrate themselves in several ways including how well you take and give direction.

Some things to consider:

1. How are you showing up? How conscious are you of your emotional energy when you are at work?

2. Do you bring high positive and constructive energy to what you do?

3. Do you display a low level of energy that suggests low enthusiasm and disinterest in what you do?

4. What is your dominant communication style?

5. How has your communication style helped or

hindered you?

6. What type of listener are you?

7. If you've not had the benefit of a 360° evaluation, make it a goal to have one conducted. If your organization does not administer 360° assessments, if you are working with an executive or career coach, they should have access to a 360° assessment tool. If none of these options are available to you, drop me a note at and I will be happy to assist you. My email address is:
Deborah@CoachDgrayYoung.com,

Excerpted and edited from YOU 3.0: A Guide to Overcoming Roadblocks for Professional Women of Color ©2015 D. Gray-Young

"What Do They Mean When They Say…?"

8 What's Your RQ?

What's your RQ - Your relationship intelligence quotient?

How strong are your relationships with influencers and key people within your organization, especially those who may influence your career trajectory?

Relationships are how we manage to accomplish anything. This is true, of course, whether we work within a company or have our own business. It's whom we know, who knows us, and what they think of us and our capabilities. Relationship building is an ongoing endeavor.

Your RQ is a considerable part of your brand. However, it's also where many people get stuck. Why? Because your RQ is central to being politically savvy, which is a pain point for many people.

Answer these questions honestly and then review the tips that follow.

- What key relationships do you have? Who are your champions?
- What key relationship(s) don't you have?
- Who are detractors? What is at issue here?
- Whom do you need to win over?

Here are some tips on building professional relationships within your organization as well as your industry.

- Build dossiers on important internal and external stakeholders. LinkedIn and Google are your best tools here. You want to get a glimpse of who they are and what their mindset could potentially be.
  - Where did they go to school?
  - What did they study?
  - Did they play sports?
  - What part of the country or world are they from?
  - What is their previous experience before joining the current organization?
  - Have they authored books or written articles for industry blogs?

These are the types of information nuggets that will help you identify a basis for conversation and begin building a professional relationship.

Next, you'll build a stakeholder map using what you learned from developing the dossiers. This process is what I use with my clients, and it is invaluable when they are interviewing for senior executive leadership positions. It makes for quite an impressive conversation.

"What Do They Mean When They Say...?"

9 Developing A Stakeholder Map

Instructions: Based on dossiers you have assembled, make an assessment of what the critical issues or concerns are likely to be for key stakeholders in your organization.

Developing dossiers is especially important to develop for those stakeholders who have direct or indirect influence over your experience and success in the organization.

What is important to note about each is what/how should their respective issues or concerns be approached from your experience, expertise, and knowledge? What experiences can you use to illustrate your expertise and knowledge?

Using the chart and scale on the following page, rank the importance of each issue for each stakeholder.

Don't know what the critical business issues are? Now is an excellent time to learn. Make sure to read and follow the instructions in chapters 10 and 11. Send me a note to let me know how it worked for you. BTW, all of this applies to business owners as well.

Legend:

1. Critical Importance	5. Not Important
3. Somewhat Important	6. Neutral

STAKEHOLDER	Responsibility/Concern	Responsibility/Concern	Responsibility/Concern	Responsibility/Concern	Responsibility/Concern

"What Do They Mean When They Say…?"

10 Always Be A Student of Your Craft

There's an adage that it's not what you know, but who you know that matters. Today's marketplace has changed that somewhat. Even for the well connected, who you know isn't enough for longevity. We see it almost every day now, thanks to 24/7 news cycles and social media outlets.

Incompetence also shows up in work product; the quality of the work that is produced. Today, the fiscal pressure of corporations is far greater than their tolerance for sloppy work.

In any case, whatever field or career you are engaged in or pursuing, be a student of your craft. Strive to be the best and being the best means studying any and everything you can about your craft, your organization and the industry you work in.

It means keeping up on how your craft and your industry are changing and evolving. It means keeping up with the needs and preferences of the end user – the end user being your consumer, customer or client - whomever ultimately uses your work product. It also means understanding the implications of related industries.

As an example, when the internet and search capabilities first emerged, publishing companies and retailers ignored this technological event. Today, the internet is ubiquitous. It is the primary way information and entertainment are distributed and accessed. In addition, it is quickly becoming the dominant way consumers purchase all goods and services including cars and mortgages. The most common way people access news, information, and entertainment today is through the internet on their mobile phone.

Represented in this brief description are monumental shifts in marketing, advertising, sales, television programming, car buying, content distribution and most of all how people communicate and socialize with each other.

To be fair, very few saw this coming. However, those who did were able to lead the transition, or at the very least, help define and explain the changes as they occurred.

Back in the day, we called these folks geeks and nerds. Today we call them visionaries. Students of their respective craft with the gift of panoramic vision; the ability to see the larger board and understand where there are missing pieces without knowing precisely what those pieces might be. However, because they are students of their craft, they will likely recognize the missing pieces when they see them.

Being a student of your craft is one of the best ways to build value around the service you provide either in your job or your business. It is the primary way, I have found, that will minimize your getting blindsided when the sand shifts beneath your feet as someone recently described the rapid change the world is currently experiencing.

When you are a student of your craft, it will allow you to spot trends and forecast not just revenue but how to adapt to what's coming around the corner.

The first step in becoming a student of your craft is of course reading. It is fundamental. A quick and easy way to stay abreast of your industry is SmartBriefs. There are dozens of them informing on dozens of industries, and they are free. You can subscribe at Smartbriefs.com. Find the briefs that will help make you smarter about what you do and how you contribute to the organization. Setting Google Alerts for industry topics, companies, and industry leaders is also an excellent way to stay abreast of your field. The good news is that you can do all of this from your phone or tablet.

Become a student of your craft and increase your value and your success. Be better prepared for what's coming, because if nothing else is true, change is constant.

Consider this:

Are you a student of your craft? Here is a quick test to find out:

1. Do you know what you don't know? Make a list

2. Are you a subject matter expert? If yes, is it a subject that is important in your current role or field?

3. How do you stay abreast of the trends and the next thing coming in your industry?

4. How are you positioned to be a leader when the new reality arrives?

Excerpted and edited from YOU 3.0: A Guide to Overcoming Roadblocks for Professional Women of Color ©2015 D. Gray-Young

"What Do They Mean When They Say…?"

11 Want to Be Taken Seriously? Take A Selfie

In the chapter, "How Do Others View You, Really?" we discussed style and attitude as the energy we show up with and how the energy we display influences others' perception of us. Another major roadblock to our success is not being taken seriously by executive leadership, colleagues, and peers.

If you are not being taken seriously in your role, there are potentially any number of reasons why. However, let's start by understanding another aspect of how you might be perceived within your organization.

Take a selfie. Not a picture of you doing something fun, but rather, a self-examination. In no more than 15 seconds, answer the following questions:

When you are at work, what are you the go-to-person for in your organization or department?

If it's more than one thing, list them. For example, are you the instant restaurant guide or music and movie critic? Are you the entertainment and celebrity know-it-all?

What issues or challenges do your peers come to you for answers or suggestions?

If you have a layer of management above you, for what do

the respective executives rely on you? Fill in the blank.

I am the go-to-person for
_____

Here is another quick selfie exercise. In 15 seconds list the 3 top trends or challenges in your industry, field or company.

The top 3 trends or challenges in my field or company are:

1. _____
2. _____
3. _____

How closely related are your two selfies? Is what you are known for and what people come to you for related to your role in the organization, your knowledge of your industry or business acumen? Or are the two completely different? You can probably see where I'm going with this.

If your answer to the first set of Selfies is not what you would like to be the go-to-person for, then for what would you want to be the go-to-person?

If you had difficulty with the second set of selfies of readily identifying the trends and challenges of your field, you also have some work to do.

If your selfies are not what you want them to be, all is not lost. There are some very deliberate steps you can take to change that; become a student of your craft. It will require you to be focused, and willing to invest in yourself.

"What Do They Mean When They Say…?"

Select an area or two that you can become a subject matter expert.

One of the ways to be taken seriously is by asking intelligent and thought-provoking questions that are based on what you have learned through research and information gathering, rather than pure curiosity. People always remember the question that made the room stop and think. However, don't overuse this approach. It could get you labeled as a smartass. You don't want that either. We're trying to eliminate, not add on obstacles.

Your Assignment:

1. Take some quiet time to record your thoughts about what you want to achieve

2. For what would you like to be the go-to-person?

3. How important is it for you to become that person?

4. What would it take for you to become that person?

5. What are the top challenges in your industry, organization, and field?

6. What resources will you use to assist you in acquiring that information?

7. Develop a plan of action to help you become that go-to-person. Don't forget to ask for help. There's no need to go it alone.

Excerpted from YOU 3.0: A Guide to Overcoming Roadblocks for Professional Women of Color. ©2015 D. Gray-Young

"What Do They Mean When They Say...?"

12 "Who's Holding Your Ladder?"

One of the roadblocks to success is not having an adequate support system. This is not uncommon for women who have been raised and trained to be self-sufficient and self-reliant. Being self-sufficient and self-reliant can work against women in general and women of color in particular in some corporate environments. What do I mean by that?

When we experience difficulty managing certain situations, asking for help is not something that occurs to us readily. Mostly, we will try to work through a situation on our own. When we can't see our way through to a successful solution or resolution, we begin looking for a way out.

Instead of looking for a way out, consider this: What does your support system look like? Who's holding your ladder? Who have you selected to be part of your inner circle, professionally and personally?

In his book, **"Who's Holding Your Ladder?"** Dr. Samuel Chand, a ministry leadership coach, recounts an experience he had while waiting in a pastor's study to be introduced to speak, that led to a poignant aha moment

He tells the story of observing a workman painting a building across the street. As he watched the man work, he noticed that the painter could not go any higher and could not stretch his arms any further to the left or right. Dr. Chand couldn't see down to the street, and so he wondered out loud, who is holding this workman's ladder?

It occurred to Dr. Chand at that moment that the workman would not and could not go any further than he was comfortable climbing or reaching. He did have room to climb to the top of the building on the ladder's extension, and in fact, he would have to do that to finish the job. However, the workman needed just one thing to help him; The workman had to have someone holding his ladder steady while he worked. He had to have help.

Dr. Chand saw this as a metaphor for leaders in ministry. When I read and studied this story, I saw it as a metaphor for effective leadership and successful living in our everyday personal and professional lives.

At the end of the day, all we want is a fair chance to demonstrate our ability. Nothing more, nothing less! So, do everything within your power to give yourself a fair advantage. Start with developing the support team you need instead of going it alone.

In her book, Sister Citizen, Melissa Harris-Perry talks about the consequences of self-reliance for Black women. The result is that Black women are less satisfied with their lives than any other group. We need to change that.

Just who and what are ladder holders, anyway?

"What Do They Mean When They Say…?"

Ladder Holders are:

Allies: An ally is someone whom you can bounce things off including ideas and not worry about being misrepresented or your ideas showing up in somebody else's work.

Do you have allies or champions within your organization?

Champions: A champion is someone who respects your work, what you contribute to the organization and the team. They are in a position to champion your talents and contributions to key stakeholders. They can help you gain the right visibility that can lead to better career building projects and assignments. Champions are like sponsors in some ways, but like all relationships, it is a relationship that is earned.

Mentors: Have you sought out a mentor? It is not the most straightforward task you will ever have, but it is one worth undertaking. Identifying a mentor should be an intentional and strategic undertaking. Mentors are not just for people just beginning their career. As your career evolves, as situations and marketplaces change, having a mentor or mentors will always be crucial.

A mentor should be someone who has navigated some terrain already. However, their job is not to hold your hand, but to provide insight and guidance. Most people who would be great mentors don't have time to be a mentor. Their plates are full and their calendars even fuller. Your responsibility as a mentee, therefore, is to be open, honest and a good listener. Your job as a mentee is to be clear about your goals and the challenges you are experiencing.

Truth Teller: In your personal life, do you have at least one truth teller? Your truth-teller should be someone whom you respect and who respects you; A person that will tell you the truth no matter what because they care about you.

It's good to have girlfriends and family members that think you are fabulous. We all need those. However, everyone has to have at least one person that will call you out or hold you accountable. I'm not talking about judgmental criticism or tearing you down to make you feel less than your greatness. I'm talking about honest, objective truth-telling because they love and respect you and are willing to risk you being angry with them over it.

What does having a support system do for you? It provides:

- Honest and objective feedback
- Guidance and counsel
- Strengthened confidence
- Exposure of capabilities to stakeholders
- Increased opportunities

Assignment #1

- Who is in your inner circle that can lend you assistance with navigating those challenging situations in your career?

- Make a list and consider your current ladder holders. If you are a manager or team leader, do you have the right skill mix on your team? Do you know what the right skill mix that is needed for your team to be successful?

- In your personal life, also consider who are your ladder holders. Should they be asked to take on the responsibility of holding your ladder steady? Perhaps they have too much on their plate with their own careers and lives.

Assignment #2:

- How do you select ladder holders? Make a list of what types of people should be a part of your ladder holding team. Be honest. Just because you love them doesn't mean they should be holding your ladder. They can have another vital role in your life.

- Begin with understanding what your guiding principles are.

Your guiding principles are those ideals or qualities that make up the foundation for everything you do; for how you live your life. Your ladder holders, whether professional or personal, should align with the most important of your principles.

Below are some examples of principles or values that might make up your foundation, but certainly take the time to define your own list.

fairness	family	service
excellence	leadership	trust
commitment	integrity	Respect

Excerpted from YOU 3.0: A Guide to Overcoming Roadblocks for Professional Women of Color. ©2015 D. Gray-Young. Chapter title and story used by permission of Dr. Samuel Chand. Chand, Samuel and Cecil Murphy. Who's Holding Your Ladder? Niles. Mall Publishing Company 2003. print

"What Do They Mean When They Say...?"

13 About That LinkedIn™ Profile

If you do not have a LinkedIn profile, read the rest of this chapter and then go straight to LinkedIn.com, sign up for a LinkedIn account and set up your profile.

LinkedIn, in case you didn't know, is the primary platform and directory of professionals in any industry and all levels of experience and achievement.

It is distinctly different from other social media channels in that it is strictly for professional and business networking. There have been sightings of people attempting to use it for more social purposes. Individuals seeking to use LinkedIn for other purposes have been met with being uninvited or muted.

That said, here are some tips and guidelines on setting up your LinkedIn profile and making effective use of the platform.

1. You must have a professional headshot in professional clothing. No bare shoulders, plunging necklines, standing in front of statues or windows. No iPhone selfies or passport pictures. A professional headshot taken by a professional photographer. You get the idea.

2. Next are your name and a brief description of what you do in bold action words. Look through profiles and make a note of those that stand out to you. What captured your attention? That's what you want; to

attract someone's professional attention. Of course, what you say under your name needs to accurately reflect what you do and what you can deliver on.

3. Following the sections as they are outlined, what is it that you want people who find you on LinkedIn to know? What are the core responsibilities of your current role? Alternatively, what are the key competencies you wish to display to attract your next opportunity? What are your most compelling accomplishments? Review several if not dozens of profiles for examples and ideas.

You can always seek out LinkedIn™ experts who will develop your profile for a fee. You can search for them on LinkedIn or conduct a general Google search.

4. Building your network and connections. This requires some thought. LinkedIn limits you to the number of invitations you can send out. Approximately 3,000, so I've been told. Therefore, you will want to be very judicious with your allotment. You will go through it quicker than you think.

5. Try to avoid sending the general invitation to connect. The temptation to do this is powerful when presented with "people you may know." This feature will simply have a "connect" button. If you click on the person's profile, find the three dots in the box that features the picture and description of the person and find the "send a personalized invitation" option.

The connections you seek should make sense for your goals. It doesn't help you to have hundreds of people in your network that are unrelated to what you do or want to do. Conversely, the person receiving your invitation should be able to discern why you are asking them to join their professional network.

BTW, if you do not have a professional picture and a clearly defined headline and description, you significantly reduce your chances of your invitations being accepted.

6. Joining groups. There are hundreds of groups on LinkedIn. Consult the group directory and identify the groups that would be helpful to you in expanding your network. There are groups for university alumni, chapter alumni, professional groups by industry and groups representing special interests.

If you elect to receive notices about posts and comments, I would suggest using a personal email address. The volume can be overwhelming. You definitely do not want a call from IT asking you about the tremendous increase in email volume.

Once you sign up and set up your profile, spend some time on the platform to get a feel for how people use it, and what types of information and articles are posted. You will begin to see how you might contribute; posting original content or sharing some business or industry news you read that you found compelling.

Any way you look at it, LinkedIn is a crucial platform for your professional brand and presence. It is now the primary resource for recruiters. It is also an essential resource for identifying business opportunities. When you Google your name, your LinkedIn profile will likely be the first item that shows up in the search results.

There is much more to know and learn about LinkedIn that could fill a book. Take advantage of the LinkedIn training videos on YouTube or seek out some of the LinkedIn experts and professionals to assist you if you need to. This is the one social networking platform on which you should be active.

14 A Final Word

The trajectory of your life and career are primarily up to you. How you show up on any given day and how well you are prepared to perform are your responsibility. Things will not always go your way. It's called life, and no, it's not always fair. Get the lesson disappointment brings and use it to strengthen your resolve. It's a test of your commitment to yourself and your goals.

When you hit a rough patch or find yourself in unfamiliar territory, reach out for help. Smart, successful people never go it alone. It's their secret weapon.

It would be great if the company you work for invests in your professional development. Ultimately, that is your responsibility, so plan to make investments in you. You are worth it.

Finally, be diligent about developing and protecting your personal and professional brand. They are one and the same. Be careful who and what you affiliate your brand. Be cognizant of how you present it and how others view it. At the end of the day, your brand – your reputation is the only currency you have.

I wish you success and balance in every area of your life.

Until next time,

Deborah

Life is about choices. What will you choose for you today?

About the Author

Deborah Gray-Young is the managing partner of D. Gray-Young, Inc., a consulting and coaching firm. Deborah is an award-winning advertising and marketing professional with three decades of experience. As an ICF certified coach, Deborah provides executive coaching services for professional women of color and the organizations that employ them.

In addition to working with senior leaders, Deborah has been lauded for her development of young professionals and helping them to grow into a successful path in advertising and marketing and other fields.

Highly regarded by colleagues, peers, and clients, Deborah is known for her strategic foresight and ability to connect the obvious and not so obvious dots. She has a keen eye for what will work and what will be short-lived. She is frequently sought out by media company CEOs, network and content producers, print and digital publishers and advertising sales executives for her point of view and counsel. Her insight has been requested by major business and industry trade publications including the Wall Street Journal, USA Today, the Washington Post, Black Enterprise and others.

Deborah has served on the advisory council of Black Life Coaches Network. She also served for 11 years on the External Advisory Council for the international market research firm Nielsen where she provided insight and counsel to executive leadership on workforce diversity and retention.

Read her full bio at www.coachdgrayyoung.com or www.dgrayyoungconsulting.com

Follow her on:
LinkedIn https://www.linkedin.com/in/dgrayyoung
Twitter: @coachdgrayyoung

Books by Deborah Gray-Young

YOU 3.0: Overcoming Roadblocks for Professional Women of Color

Professional women of color experience a double-edged bias – gender and race - that has now mutated the historical stereotypes into 21st-century archetypes. What are the stereotypes and how do we manage them and the resultant experiences? These are just some of the roadblocks that must be overcome.

Available on Amazon, Kindle, and BarnesandNoble.com

The Young Professional's Handbook: Some Things You Need to Know Before and After You Get the Job.

A primer for young men and women entering the professional workforce.

Available on Amazon, Kindle, and BarnesandNoble.com

D. Gray-Young Workshops, Webinars and Speaking Engagements

For workshops, webinars, and speaking engagements contact Deborah at:

872-228-7068
Deborah@Coachdgrayyoung.com or
Deborah@DGrayYoungConsulting.com

- **How Do Others View You, Really?** Your image is more than how you look. Are you in control of your professional image? Are you conscious of the quality and level of energy you bring to everything you do? The key to being taken seriously is understanding how you are perceived.

- **What Do They Mean When They Say…?** Decoding Performance Evaluation Speak. Based on the book of the same title, explores some of the common phrases attached to this question and strategies to address them.

- **How to be Politically Savvy on Your Own Terms** What does it mean to be politically savvy and how to acquire it. Why it's necessary to be politically savvy.

- **What's Your RQ?** Your professional relationship intelligence quotient. Whom do you know and who knows you? A guide to building relationships with stakeholders and building stakeholder maps

- **When You're the Only One**: Effective strategies when you are the only woman or person of color in the room

- **The Platinum Rule:** Do unto others as they would have others do unto them.

- **Who's Holding Your Ladder?** How to assemble the right support team for your personal and professional life.

- **The Types that Bind Us.** Presented in 2 parts. Stereotypes are the #1 challenge for women of color. Understand the origins of stereotypes and how they are impacting your personal and professional life

From **The Young Professional's Handbook:**

- **How to be a Student of Your Craft.** The fundamental steps to take and habits to form early in one's career to increase success.

- **Managing Up.** The most important skill you will ever develop; how to manage the levels of management above you.

- **Developing Informed Questions.** It's well thought-out and informed questions that make for a memorable interview and impressive conversations with stakeholders.

"What Do They Mean When They Say…?"

What People Say About Deborah

Deborah, I want you to know how much I appreciate working with you. The suggestions, insight, and guidance you have given me these past few months are invaluable.

You have and continue to make a difference in my life. I appreciate you and please don't ever stop your awesomeness!

Managing Director, Fortune 500 Transportation & Logistics company

Deborah, You inspired me to really open up and go after what I deserve and want out of my career. So six months later I did just that. I wanted to share my news with you and let you know how a short period of time with you had a lifetime impact. You have a friend for life. Thank you!

Promoted from Claims Account Executive to Regional Director, Fortune 500 Insurance Company

Hi Deborah,
Your work is so important. After our sessions, I looked at myself in a different way – a more positive and powerful way… THANK YOU for listening and being honest with me. I am confident that your work can change people in a very positive way -- which can create more success in the world.

Marketing Communications Professional, NYC & Washington, DC

What People Say About Deborah

"...As a result of her coaching, I have stretched my thinking and capacity, developed a more cohesive relationship with my team and strengthened my effectiveness in leading, communicating and guiding.

While I have grown professionally, I have also grown personally. Deborah has helped me to bring balance to my life, prioritize and regain my passion. She has the ability to actively listen, ask the right questions and leave you with helpful insights, ideas, and questions to ponder, ultimately leading you to make a well-thought-out decision. The value and benefit are immeasurable... It is one of the best investments I have made.

EVP of Sales, Los Angeles, CA

Deborah has been a go-to professional coach for national business and professional networking events produced by Black Enterprise. She is authentic and committed to both delivering results and holding clients accountable for delivering their own.

Deborah is more than a difference-maker; she creates difference-makers.

Alfred Edmonds, Jr., SVP, Executive Editor At large, Black Enterprise Magazine, Relationship Educator

"What Do They Mean When They Say...?"

Cover Design: Lynn Winston, Powell Graphics & Communications, Chicago

Back cover Photography: Victor Powell Photography, Chicago

www.ingramcontent.com/pod-product-compliance
Lightning Source LLC
Chambersburg PA
CBHW031212090426
42736CB00009B/882